Willy Ronis
Sundays by the River

Willy Ronis
Sundays by the River

Foreword by Noël Simsolo

Smithsonian Institution Press
Washington, D.C.

Originally published in Italian in 1994
by Federico Motta Editore

Published 1999 in the United States of America
by Smithsonian Institution Press
in association with Federico Motta Editore, Milan

Translation from French and Italian by Renata Treitel

Library of Congress Cataloging-in-Publication Data

Ronis, Willy, 1910–
    [Sorties du dimanche. English]
    Sundays by the river / Willy Ronis : text by Noël
Simsolo]
        p.   cm. — (Motta fotografia)
    Translation of Sorties du dimanche (never published in
original French).
    ISBN 1-56098-887-8 (alk. paper)
    1. Paris Region (France)—Pictorial works. 2. Paris
Region (France)—Social life and customs—Pictorial works.
3. French—Recreation—France—Seine River—Pictorial
works. I. Title. II. Series.
    DC715.R67   1999
    944′.36—dc21   98-47592

06 05 04 03 02 01 00 99   5 4 3 2 1

Printed by Arti Grafiche Motta, Milan
Manufactured in Italy, not at government expense

Sundays by the River

After the war, I still remember, the French used to listen to the warm voice of Yves Montand, the son of an Italian emigrant, streaming out of the loudspeakers of the wireless radio and singing a refrain of which the first couplet ended with a contagious profession of faith:

Mais le dimanche, mais le dimanche,
Moi, je me sens bien, bien, bien,
Car je ne fais rien, rien, rien . . .

But on Sunday, on Sunday,
I feel so well, well, well
'cause I'm free, free, free . . .

I was not quite ten years old and happily repeated the refrain out of a desire to parrot like a third-rate actor. My artless imitation and my immature voice entertained my neighbors and sometimes pleased passersby on that day of leisure. They smiled, listening to my performance, exchanged accomplices' looks with my mother, and, at times, picked up the same lines to whistle them in unison, in a long, conspiratorial echo, while they kept walking on the pavements of the city.

In those days Sundays seemed to count more than anything else. One would not leave on the weekend, and the TV channels catered to the wealthy. Back then, Paris teemed with people. The workers took advantage of their twenty-four hour respite to breathe the air of the streets, smiling like a king relieved from the importunities of his courtiers. It was the furtive cessation of despair, anxieties, and regrets: the right to live a moment for oneself, without egoism or hatred, to experience a simple and modest peace before returning to the factory or the office the next day.

For them, the day of the Lord was, above all, the opportunity to merge with Paris, to window-shop at luxury department stores, to search for green in the public gardens, and to sit at the edge of the water.

Witnesses to those times loved the spectacle of that placid wandering. It proved, to all appearances, the resumption of a calm, normal life, despite colonial problems in Indochina, the frequency of violent strikes, and the alarming rumors of a new international conflict in the future.

In those days the new realism and popular culture offered strong behavioral models to the people. The great myths about life's small joys found therein an echo of the Popular Front because Sunday's entertainment was considered to be a well-deserved reward after the hard work of the week.

In 1936 the actor Jean Gabin was already dancing on the banks of the Marne and singing: "When one walks beside the water." The film was called *La belle équipe* (in English *They Were Five*). It conformed to the fashion of poetic realism and carried, with ambiguity, the hope of tomorrows that sing for the working class.

The images of the peaceful water, that popular singer, and easygoing workers had become, under the German occupation, a symbol. Water linked to happiness and freedom. An association that went without saying. . . .

Man has always loved to relax by rivers. . . .

Memories are made of clinging smells and numerous noises. Hearing and the sense of smell impregnate the cells of our brains tenaciously. Images fade more quickly. They constitute a vague mixture on the wrong side of our memories. One betrays oneself when one wants to piece them together in one's mind. Everything gets distorted by the subjectivity of the experienced sensation. Dream mingles with reality.

We never cease to reinvent mental images that pursue us throughout our lives. Also, photography allows us to preserve in our minds a few of the most tangible signs that rekindle one moment of our past or to relive a fleeting emotion.

My childhood was branded by those rectangles in black and white, printed on the glossy paper of magazines, traced on the porous paper of public posters, or printed with jagged edges by the amateur photographer of the neighborhood so that the photographs could decorate the precious family album.

In the past our parents were all Sunday photographers. Until the invention of the camcorder, the twentieth century was the century of the snapshot.

I look at the pictures and remember. . . .

In those days workers considered Sunday to be a day on which one had to be clean and respectable. In the morning, not too early, they usually washed themselves carefully in front of the kitchen sink or bent over an enameled basin, for bathrooms were very scarce.

Then they dressed in immaculate clothes, put on polished shoes, and took great care with their hair.

After that, staying at home was out of the question. Going out was a duty. Smelling of good soap and dressed in impeccable clothes, they strolled leisurely through town. I still see them leisurely strolling . . . proud and gentle, early in the afternoon, especially in the spring, when a light breeze cooled the temples and softened the breathing. . . .

If the movie theater was a goal for their stroll, like a visit to the cemetery or family reunions, the main objective was often to go for a breath of fresh air at the edge of the water. When the weather permitted, they loved to linger by the river or its tributaries in the suburbs.

For them, the day was placed under the sign of water.

Water.

Water attracts man from time immemorial. Teachers have taught that man's life began there. The origin of life is aquatic.

Mankind developed side by side with amphibians and fish. Some learned scientists have thus explained that the human species was born in the blue-green between two depths. Later, bones, cartilage, and lungs differentiated us from the rest of the sea animals. Earth received us. But we are orphans of the waves.

Furthermore, water meant survival for the first adventurers of our planet. Their heavy, apelike bodies could not survive without drinking water. After that, they understood the other uses that water could have for them and they learned to use it in the best possible way.

When the tribe wandered too far from the beaches, the chief always looked for a river or stream to set up camp. The first mortal combats took place for the possession or defense of that kind of territory, where water flowed for man to drink.

Later, they built villages, then cities, by the rivers or by the sea. All civilizations were born this way. Polytheistic religions all had their god of water, who was more important than Bacchus and Eros.

Centuries have passed, but an unstoppable force lures man continually to come and to gaze at the water.

Eternal fascination without restraint. A symbol of life that man associates quite obviously with the peace of Sundays, like an homage to the element from which he originates. This is due perhaps to the organic need to feel alive and in tune with our original nature, where everything responds to a less explicit drive: one of the subjects dear to psychoanalysts. . . .

Whatever the reasons or habit, man heads for the water, and there he meditates, breathes, collects his thoughts, or finds himself again.

Right next to the great mystery . . . in an ineffable mysticism without divinity. A meditation not identified with any particular creed.

The view of a fountain, an artificial lake, a narrow stream, or an unleashed ocean causes a similar feeling of plenitude and humility in the observer. To spend one Sunday at the edge of the water—a usual theme for poets, impressionistic painters, or composers of popular songs—is a way to give oneself a mass in secret.

It does not matter if one attends that intimate ritual in the company of friends, a girlfriend, children, or parents. The holiday can forge its own plan, a chamber orchestra can play sonatas, the guitarist can regale his friends, or the street peddler can shout happily, the better to sell his clandestine merchandise. It will not do. By the water communion becomes as imperative for the solitary as for the organized group. Communion does not necessarily last for hours. One moment may be enough to touch with one's finger the feeling of well-being. Beside the water.

In the middle of Paris, winding across an architecture of tightly fitted stones or rough concrete of anonymous houses or famous monuments, of trees with red leaves due to carbon monoxide fumes or low walls covered with graffiti, the Seine continues calmly to excavate the clay in the belly of the city.

From time immemorial the Seine has attracted people of all conditions and all ages. They have remained faithful to it. That rite persists even today. Certainly, people do not wear beautiful clothes anymore on the day of leisure. On the contrary, it is almost compulsory to dress down. From one year to the next, customs change, anxiety about the future grows, and the street causes more and more fear. But the river always has companions on its banks.

Water is the only free entertainment for the poor or thrifty. The lazier ones, or those still tired from the rhythm of the factory, love to fall asleep by the river. Others cast their fishing lines hoping to bring back something to fry. Some dream of legends by the river, where sea monsters, tiny sirens, and divers in full gear come across hypothetical blue whales, lost between the Pont Alexandre III and the Cathedral of Notre Dame. Others, less imaginative, are content to settle for the river as a primordial element of decor the better to appreciate a sunny breakfast on the grass, under the arbor of a house, or in the midst of the musical noise of a café.

There is also the courageous athlete who stirs the wave with the regulated handling of his oars, or those who enjoy running on the riverbanks, trying to carry away the victory of a local challenge sponsored by a brand of aperitif and a municipal council.

Only a few stubborn pelota players ignore the river temporarily, giving themselves entirely to their passion for the game in the cool shade of a fisherman's café.

But always, as long as the world is what it is, couples will come to stretch out by the river's side, astonished, feverish, or calm, their eyes half closed, their hearts beating with tenderness or sexual impatience, with a thousand desires still held back by a feeling of purity that they have attained at last and, above all, convinced that this way time has stopped so that their love will really last until the end of the world.

Time stops. Photographs. Displays of photographic proofs come from different epochs. Memories are mental pictures; one tries frantically to make them move so as to relive yesterday's emotion. Or to invent it.

Water, even stagnant water, invariably moves. Indeed, it is the photograph that makes water motionless, as is always the case for any movement. That of the runner. That of the regatta lover. That of the ball thrower. That of the singer happy to regale his friends of the moment. That of a lonely young girl gathering flowers in the meadow between the wild river and the inhumane factory. That of the painter applying glaze on the copy in oils of the landscape that he wants so much to make his own with brushes and imagination. That of the barge flying past toward an unknown destination with reckless children on board, who play an endless adventure. That of the guitarist intent on seduction. That of the dancer who boldly attempts, as in one photograph in this book, to make two docile and very young girls, totally absorbed for fear that a clumsy gesture might break the magic, twirl around to the syncopated rhythms of the boogie-woogie. Restaurant keepers and musicians are among the few who dare work on Sundays.

So many frozen images of a motionless kaleidoscope, striking sudden poses like teenagers in bathing suits or traditional clothes. They are waiting for the order from the amateur photographer to breathe and laugh again without worry.

But here the game is totally different. One holds one's breath and lends a semblance of cessation of life to one's smiling body to perpetuate an artist's or one's own scrupulously staged image forever. Beautiful comedy, whereas water never submits itself. Water is not itself anymore in the frozen image that records its passing before the lens. . . . Caught on film, water is dead. It is a play of light or a photographer's skill that lends to water the pretense of movement at rest.

Looking at these pictures, taken over time, I find myself thinking that Willy Ronis must detest folklore and its parade of picturesque effects. He prefers to steal a few small scraps of reality that, once stripped of their temporal information (clothes, hairdos, details of urban decor), desire nothing more than the proof of man's attitudes and feelings, which persist in the face of what is more powerful. At the water's edge, the individual lets the need to experience fragments of happiness pierce his deepest secrets, scraps of happiness, brittle like a child's illusion, because a deep void can break that feeling into smithereens in the sun of Sundays.

It seems to me also that the characters captured in these pictures allow a glimpse of their everyday condition, a belonging to nature and an irrepressible need to rejoin the universal tapestry.

In French, *ne rien faire* (to do nothing or pleasant idleness) can sometimes mean *se la couler douce* (to have a good time). But the lyrics sung by Yves Montand are wrong. To do nothing is impossible. Like water that never stops moving, man functions even at rest. His organs stir. His eye perceives the glow of light, the silhouette of his fellow creatures, and the slow waltz of the wave. In his head thoughts clash against each other. Even when he is dozing. If, in following the flow of water, he rediscovers that he is part of the cosmos, his social and physical reality remains nailed to his brain.

We feel that that reality perturbs somewhat the silent and peaceful magic that the meticulous photographer always likes to capture together with life's moment.

Nevertheless, behind the glossy mirror of an exceptional negative, the many secret desires and failed anxieties never cease to acknowledge themselves.

What is more readable is the revelation of the desire to fill the day well, either by carousing or tanning oneself, as if one had to bring back a trophy of the Sunday feast: a stuffed bear, a golden skin, a promise of marriage, a confirmation of a friendship, a full belly, or the tipsiness of white wine. Briefly, beyond pleasure or the pretense thereof, each person wants to belong at all costs to the society that has developed around the water and with which it has become imperative for him to live, for better or for worse. Otherwise, one lingers on the bank forever, anchored before the waves, like the tramps who live under the bridges.

For that reason, on that day, prisoner of the notion that he too is a social creature, a person looks only at water. He observes the other. The others. His doubles. Angels, devils, or innocents. . . . And he judges them, alas. . . .

If he is on a ferry, his eyes slightly taunt those who remain on the riverbank.

If he is on the riverbank, he observes with envy, jealousy, or irony those who benefit from riverboats.

Even the groups relaxing in front of the water do not try very hard to communicate with one another. Rather, they form strange flower beds of isolated humanity. If they hug or smile at one another or speak among friends, they avoid to the utmost any contact with others, as if, here, they have found again an atavistic need to protect or to defend their bit of territory near the river.

They do not know that each is at the same time a spectacle for the other. The happiness of lovers, the hopes of a couple accompanied by a baby in its carriage, the joy of a family reunited for a Sunday together, or the perseverance of a painter to recreate in another medium what he sees—these are the supreme attractions of a holiday where desire contends with tolerance.

Despite the smothered sneering, the tooth grinding quickly suppressed, and the tense distress of accepting one's disappointed hopes, truce tarries on that day. One does not quarrel on the riverbank, even when each has his own opinion.

Only the elderly seem indifferent to everything. They look inward. They have so many memories that they have become mummified, desiring to filter those memories through the sieve of happiness.

And then, happily, there are the children. Always the children. . . .

More fond of the water than anyone else on Earth.

The children. . . .

And yet vacillating between the sand of the public garden and the aquatic miracles. The children, asleep after their bottle and deep in the opaque dreams of their prebirth memories. The children, looked upon with tenderness, anxiety, and some distress by the adults, who are nostalgic for the special condition of childhood, at the margin of social duties.

A child sees everything beneath appearances. When he leans on the rail of a ferry and looks at the Eiffel Tower, his mind organizes a climb of the iron monster, to which dangerous sharks must protect the approach.

In a group children share the roles of knights, just kings, wicked viziers, or princesses, and they incorporate the waves into their fantastic tale.

If they do not have the chance to stroll with their families, they look for a playmate to perform all the daring exploits, such as climbing the crossbar of a goalpost and thinking they can catch an airplane in flight or a bird on the wing, and, finally, if their lives unfold on the river itself, the barge within a string of barges becomes the ground for games of possession, car trips, treks across the desert, or car races.

The child lives in the instant, whether the instant is photographic or not.

But the child never forgets Sundays by the river.

Noël Simsolo

Photographs